GRIZZLIES

A TRUE BOOK

by

Emilie U. Lepthien

Children's Press®
A Division of Grolier Publishing
New York London Hong Kong Sydney
Danbury, Connecticut

To my parents,
with whom I met
the grizzlies in
Yellowstone.

Reading Consultant
Linda Cornwell
Learning Resource Consultant
Indiana Department of
Education

A grizzly cub

Library of Congress Cataloging-in-Publication Data

Lepthien, Emilie U., (Emilie Utteg)
   Grizzlies / by Emilie U. Lepthien.
      p.   cm. — (A true book)
   Includes index.
   Summary: Describes the physical characteristics and habits of the
North American brown bear known as the grizzly.
   ISBN 0-516-20159-X (lib. bdg.)   ISBN 0-516-26100-2 (pbk.)
   1. Grizzly bear—Juvenile literature. [1. Grizzly bear. 2. Bears.]
I. Title. II. Series.
[QL737.C27L455   1996]
699.74'446—dc20   96-14033
                                                                          CIP
                                                                          AC

Contents

What Are Grizzlies?

Brown bears, the species *Ursus arctos*, are found across the Northern Hemisphere. They live in North America, Europe, and Asia.

In North America, there are two subspecies of brown bear. One type lives on a few islands off the coast of Alaska. Its scientific name is *Ursus arctos middendorfi*. This bear is commonly known as the Kodiak brown bear.

The other type of North American brown bear is *Ursus arctos horribilis*—the grizzly.

About 50,000 grizzly bears live in North America. Most live in Alaska or Canada.

A grizzly bear in Alaska

The grizzly bear is named for its fur, which may look streaked with gray, or "grizzled."

About 800 to 900 grizzlies live in the Rocky Mountains of Washington, Idaho, Montana, Wyoming, and Colorado.

The grizzly gets its name from the silver-tipped hairs of its coat, which give it a "grizzled" appearance.

The Mighty Grizzly

Grizzlies have large heads and very powerful jaws. Over their shoulders, they have a hump of muscle and fat. Their bodies are huge and bulky.

Grizzlies are 6 to 8 feet (1.8 to 2.5 meters) long. They weigh from 400 to 500 pounds (180 to 225 kilograms).

Grizzlies have very powerful jaws (above). An adult male grizzly may weigh as much as 500 pounds (225 kilograms) (right).

A family of grizzlies along a river in Alaska

Males continue to gain weight throughout their lives. Males are called *boars*. Females are smaller and weigh less. They are called *sows*.

Coats
of Many Colors

Although they are called "brown bears," grizzlies actually may be brown, black, or blond—or a mixture of these colors.

Grizzly bears have flat feet that allow them to stand upright.

Grizzly bears have short legs. Their flat feet enable them to stand upright. Each foot has five toes wth long, curving

Grizzlies showing
their claws

claws. The claws on their
forepaws can be used for dig-
ging as well as for fighting. The
claws can be partially retracted.

As big and heavy as they are, grizzlies can run fast. They sprint at 35 miles (56 kilometers) per hour.

A grizzly-bear cub on the run

Grizzlies have keen eyes and ears (left). When they swim, grizzlies hate getting their ears wet (above).

Grizzlies have good vision and hearing. They have an acute sense of smell. When they swim, they dislike getting their ears wet. Grizzlies are considered to be highly intelligent animals.

Grizzly Diet

During the summer and fall, grizzlies must eat as much as 80 to 90 pounds (36 to 40 kg) of food each day. This is to prepare for winter and hibernation.

Plants make up 75 percent of their diet. Their heavy molars, like those of other plant eaters, are good for crushing plant

A grizzly feeding on berries

material. Grizzlies especially like sedges, berries, nuts, roots, and tubers. They seem to sense when plants are ripest and at their most nutritious.

Though their teeth are not specialized for meat-eating, grizzlies do have pointed canine teeth to help them catch and kill such prey as fish and small animals.

TEETH
that
Tell a Tale

A grizzly bear's teeth grow throughout the bear's life. Scientists have tranquilized brown bears to study their teeth. While the bear is asleep, the scientists extract a small premolar tooth without

harming the bear. Then, they study thin slices of this tooth under a microscope. Tiny growth rings can be seen and counted. The number of rings helps determine the bear's age.

Fishing

It's fun to watch grizzlies fish for food. Brown bears gather along rivers where salmon come to spawn. The falls on the McNeil River in Alaska are a favorite fishing and observation spot.

The biggest male bears get the best fishing spots. The method of fishing is different

Every grizzly has its own way of catching fish.

with each bear. Some bears stand on the bank, watching and waiting to swipe a salmon swimming upstream.

Others wade out into the water to catch their prey. To catch a fish, a bear may use its mouth, its forepaws, or both mouth and forepaws.

Some bears "snorkel." While wading in the river, a grizzly puts its head into the water. Often, a bear snorkels with only its ears above water. When it sees a fish, it pounces on it, grabbing it in its mouth.

When salmon are abundant and the fishing is good, grizzlies eat only their favorite

A grizzly bear pounces on a fish (left). A grizzly eats a freshly caught salmon (right).

parts of the fish—the head, skin, and part of the body. Young bears who don't have their own fishing spots eat what is discarded. Usually, the

23

The younger bears get to eat whatever is discarded by the older bears.

liver, intestines, and stomach are left for foxes and gulls.

Grizzlies also catch trout and other fish in streams and rivers.

Each grizzly eats at least a dozen fish a day during the short fishing season. The bears must eat enough to sustain them through hibernation.

Hibernation

Grizzlies hibernate. When cold weather sets in, they live in dens. Some bears choose a cave. Others dig dens under trees or in hillsides. In very cold climates, grizzlies hibernate from October to April or May. While hibernating, the bears do not eat or drink.

In the summer and fall, grizzlies store up lots of fat under their hides so that they will keep warm during their winter hibernation.

By hibernation time, grizzlies may have built up 6 to 10 inches (5 to 25 centimeters) of fat under their hides. During hibernation, the grizzly's body temperature drops to less than 10 degrees Fahrenheit (5 degrees Celsius). Its heart rate drops from 40 beats a minute to 8 beats a minute.

A grizzly in its den

Reproduction

The normal life span for brown bears is about 30 years. Females do not mate until they are five years old.

Grizzlies mate in June or July. Birth of the cubs occurs early the next year, when the mother is in her den.

Female grizzlies usually give birth to one or two tiny cubs.

Ten-day-old grizzly cubs

Sometimes grizzlies have three or even four cubs at a time. Each cub weighs between 10 ounces (280 grams) and a pound (450 grams).

When the cubs first come out of the mother's womb,

their eyes are still closed and they are helpless. They look naked, but they are covered with a coat of very fine hair.

The cubs don't leave the den until they have thick coats of fur and their eyes are open. Mother's milk is rich in fat, so the nursing cubs grow rapidly.

The cubs stay with their mother for two or three years. Females usually have cubs every third year, except in places where the climate is especially harsh.

A three-month-old
grizzly cub (right)
A mother grizzly nursing
her cubs (middle)
Mother and cubs (bottom)

Play

Grizzly cubs are full of energy. They love to play. They enjoy sliding down snowbanks and rough-housing with their brothers and sisters. The cubs push and shove each other, tumbling and rolling around. They stand on their hind legs and bite each other's necks.

Play-fighting helps grizzly cubs learn skills they will need as adults.

This kind of play teaches them the hunting and fighting skills they will need as adults. If a sow has just one cub, she plays with it.

National Parks

Black and brown bears, including grizzlies, live in several United States national parks. In the 1930s, nightly bear feedings were held at hotels in Yellowstone and Yosemite national parks. Visitors sat in bleachers to watch the bears eat while park rangers provided commentaries.

A grizzly begging for food

The feedings were very popular with both tourists and bears, but the bears lost their fear of humans. Soon they begged for food at the road-sides. Tourists ignored signs that said "Do Not Feed the Bears." They forgot that the bears were not tame, and some people were badly injured.

When park officials decided to close the feeding sites, wildlife researchers urged the National Park Service to phase them out gradually. This would give the bears time to adjust to finding their own food. However, the researchers were overruled, and the sites were closed in 1971.

Grizzly bears at a garbage
dump in Alaska

Hundreds of bears, depen-
dent on "handouts," starved.
They did not know how to
search for natural food. Many
others were shot as they
foraged outside the parks.

A female grizzly
defending her cubs

Most grizzly bears stay away from humans. But grizzlies are ferocious when defending themselves or their young. Sometimes, looking for food, they attack campsites. People have been attacked and injured or killed by hungry grizzlies. Grizzlies may also prey on cattle or sheep. Clearly, farmers have mixed feelings about grizzly bears.

The National Park Service has considered setting up

A grizzly cub at Katmai
National Park in Alaska

new feeding sites in the back
country where grizzlies now
live. But no decision has been
reached.

The Future of Grizzlies

Over time, the grizzly has lost much of its natural habitat in North America. People wanted the land for industry or agriculture.

Today, however, in every state except Alaska, the grizzly is classified as a threatened species. This means that it is

A grizzly bear at a zoo

protected by laws and conservation programs. Hopefully, its numbers will increase and the mighty grizzly will never vanish from our woods and forests.

A young grizzly
in an Alaskan
meadow (above)
Grizzly mother
and cubs (right)

To Find Out More

Here are some additional resources to help you learn more about grizzlies.

 **Books**

 **Organizations**

Barrett, N.S., **Picture Library: Bears.** 1988. Franklin Watts.

Graham, Ada and Frank, **An Audubon Reader: Bears in the Wild.** 1981. Delacorte Press.

Greenland, Caroline, **Nature's Children: Black Bears.** 1986. Grolier.

Johnson, Fred, **The Big Bears.** 1973. American Wildlife Federation.

National Park Service Office of Public Inquiries
P.O. Box 37127
Washington, DC 20013
202-208-4747

Bear Watch
Suite #201
1472 Commercial Drive
Vancouver, British Columbia, V5T 2J6
1-800-836-5501
http://www2.helix.net/~ bearwtch/

The Great Bear Foundation
P.O. Box 1289
Bozeman, MT 59715-1289
1-800-822-6525
406-586-6103 (fax)
E-mail: greatbears@aol.com

Grizzly Bear Recovery
U.S. Fish and
Wildlife Service
P.O. Box 5127
Missoula, MT 59806

North American Bear Society
3875 North 44th Street, Suite 102
Phoenix, AZ 85018
602-829-0486

Online Sites

Brown and Grizzly Bears
http://www2.portage.net/~dmiddlet/bears/brown.html

World Society for the Protection of Animals
http:/www.ecology.com/WSPA/wspa.html

The International Association for Bear Research and Management
E-mail: sterling@fishgame.state.ak.us

The Nature Conservancy
http://www.abi.org/tnc/tnc.html

The Sierra Club
http://www.sierraclub.org/

The Yellowstone Grizzly Foundation
http://www.desktop.org/ygf

Important Words

abundant plentiful

acute very sensitive

canines pointed teeth meant for ripping meat

climate the average weather conditions of a region over a period of years

conservation the process of helping to preserve endangered wildlife

forage to search for food

grizzled streaked or mixed with gray

hibernate to spend the winter sleeping

molars flat teeth meant for grinding

nutritious relating to foods that help an animal or plant stay healthy and grow

retracted pulled in

species a group of living things that are alike and that are able to breed with one another

Index

Meet the Author

Emilie U. Lepthien received her B.A. and M.S. degrees and certificate in school administration from Northwestern University. She taught upper-grade science and social studies, and was a school principal in Chicago, Illinois, for twenty years. For Children's Press, she has written books in the *Enchantment of the World*, *True Book*, and *America the Beautiful* series.